ON
CAB DRIVERS
SHOPKEEPERS
and STRANGERS

ISRAEL
WHAT A
COUNTRY!

TZVIA EHRLICH-KLEIN

FELDHEIM PUBLISHERS
JERUSALEM   NEW YORK

Most of these stories first appeared in the *Jewish Tribune* of London, England. I gratefully acknowledge their kind permission to reprint them in this book.

The author will be very happy to receive readers' personal stories about the beauty of life in Israel. They can be sent to:

Tzvia Ehrlich-Klein
Arzei HaBirah 49, Apt. 32
Jerusalem, Israel

First published 2002

ISBN 1-58330-543-2

FELDHEIM PUBLISHERS
POB 35002 / Jerusalem, Israel

202 Airport Executive Park
Nanuet, NY 10954

www.feldheim.com

Printed in Israel

Acknowledgments

My deepest, heartfelt thanks and appreciation:

* To the publishers and editors of the *Jewish Tribune* of London, England, for printing my "Only in Israel" articles in their excellent newspaper for these many years, and for allowing me to expand the articles' audience by including them in this book;

* To Feldheim Publishers, for their continuous support in bringing to the public an awareness of the beauty and importance of living in our Land;

* To Sarah Weber, for her ability to see the beauty of life in Israel, for sharing her many experiences with me, and for originally encouraging me to send my "Only in Israel" articles to the *Jewish Tribune* of London;

* To the many people who have taken the time and trouble to call or write to me to share their first-hand Life in Israel stories;

* To Shifra Slater, for advising me on how to transliterate beautiful Hebrew words into an English spelling;

* To my father, Cantor Lawrence Ehrlich, for

making it possible for me to be here, living every day in the holy Land of Israel, and for instilling in me the capacity to understand, appreciate, and love our Heritage, our People, and our Land, and to his wife, Cecile Pincus Ehrlich, for standing beside him these many years with concern, devotion, and love.

I am overwhelmed at the depth of gratitude I owe to the Almighty for His constant kindness and generosity to me, and for His goodness in allowing me to share with others the beauty and joy of being, and living, in His holy Land.

May all of His children always see the good in His Land, and always enjoy the privilege of being here.

Contents

Part I: Drivers

Part II: Shopkeepers

6

Part III: "Strangers"

Introduction

Our Sages say, "Even the [mundane] conversations of the people who live in the Land of Israel are Torah" (*Vayikra Rabba* 34:7).

Our Sages sure knew what they were talking about! Every day here in Israel is an education, if you keep your eyes and ears open. It's just a question of what you notice.

What a country! And what a People! "There is no joy other than in dwelling in the Land of Israel," says the Or HaChaim (*Ki Savo* 21).

There certainly is never a dull moment here, as these true stories demonstrate.

By the same author:

- On Busdrivers, Dreidels, and Orange Juice
- Happy Hints for a Successful Aliyah
- A Children's Treasury of Sephardic Tales
- Salt, Pepper and Eternity
- To Dwell in the Palace (ed.)

Part I:
Drivers

A Regular Bus Trip

I got to my bus stop late this morning, on my way to work.

Finally the #10 bus came to "my" bus stop, about six or seven minutes later than I did. As I boarded the almost-empty bus, I said to the driver, "*Baruch HaShem*. I thought I had missed the bus!"

A *Chassidishe* male passenger in his thirties answered, "We went around in a different way, on a different street, through Meah She'arim."

The bus driver looked at the passenger through his rear-view mirror and asked, "Why didn't you tell me that we shouldn't

10

have turned down that street? I know this route? I'm a usual #10 driver?" (I guess he was new to this route, possibly filling in for a sick #10 driver or something.)

The passenger merely smiled and sort of mumbled that he hadn't wanted to embarrass him. (I now knew why there were only six other passengers in addition to myself in a bus that usually contained at least ten to twenty people at that hour!)

The bus driver, who was now stopped at a red light, turned in his seat to face the *Chassidishe* man, and asked him, "So how do the people from Meah She'arim get all the way to the bus stop at Zvill? It's a long walk!"

The light then changed back to green, and the driver turned around in his seat, and just continued driving along....

I was amazed that it was possible for a bus driver to go the wrong way on his bus route, and I thoroughly enjoyed the fact that such a crazy, funny thing could happen – and the fact that no one acted as if it was the end of the world.

I was also impressed that, when his mistake was pointed out to him, the bus driver's reaction was merely concern that people had to walk farther to reach the real, correct bus route than they would have had to on his innovative one.

I also liked the idea of the *Chassidishe* man getting involved in the conversation between the bus driver and me, and the fact that he was so concerned for the feelings of a bus driver that he wouldn't embarrass him in public unnecessarily. (The fact that I could witness such a good, down-to-earth lesson in proper behavior so early in the morning was also delightful.)

But perhaps what I liked best of all was that I could start my day in such an amazingly complete way – humor and *mussar* all at once.

A bus trip in Israel.

Then there is the bus-riding story of my friend Chaya S., who was returning to her home in the Mattersdorf neighborhood of Jerusalem from a shopping expedition downtown.

The #3 bus she was on, which was quite full of people, was traveling down Rehov Yechezkel, a very narrow, but busy, street.

Suddenly the bus driver pulled the entire bus onto the sidewalk. Putting it into "park," he jumped out of the bus, and ran over to a large metal *tzedaka* box that was mounted on a light-pole on the sidewalk (yes, a city light-pole).

A bus-full of passengers waiting, the bus driver quickly dumped a few coins into the *tzedaka* box, and then returned to his bus.

He shifted the bus out of "park," and everybody continued on their way.

Of course, no one even thought to say anything... because, after all, what was there to say? Isn't it nice to have a bus driver who keeps his priorities straight?

This bus story took place over a year ago on the #11 bus from the Ramat Shlomo neighborhood of Jerusalem.

A friend, Miriam L., was one of the first

passengers on the bus that day since she lives near the first bus stop of the #11 route. She thus was able to get the seat right behind the bus driver — the perfect seat for seeing and hearing much of what goes on in a bus....

After traveling past only a few bus stops, a little boy climbed onto the bus and sat down across the aisle from Miriam — i.e., in easy view of both my friend and the bus driver.

Two or three bus stops later, this little boy suddenly burst into tears. And, as the bus was slowly meandering through the residential streets, he continued to cry and cry and cry.

By the next bus stop, the driver turned around in his seat, and asked the little boy, "Why are you crying so hard? What is wrong?"

The sobbing little boy answered that he had been given very specific directions by his mother regarding when he should get off the bus, which way he should walk, and how to get to where he was supposed to go. But he no longer remembered anymore what his mother had said to do nor where he was supposed to get off the bus.

Without a word to anyone, or a comment of any kind, the bus driver turned the entire bus around and returned to the child's home. He then opened the bus's doors and told the little boy to hurry and ask his mother for directions again, and then to hurry back.

Meanwhile the bus driver again turned his (big, city) bus around in order to be heading in the right direction when the child returned. He then proceeded to explain the whole story to his perplexed passengers.

Of course, being Israel, no one complained or protested this disruption in the regular scheduling of public transportation. Everyone just waited for the little boy to come back to the bus and climb aboard.

Which he soon did.

And then the bus just drove off again, continuing on its regular route.

Maybe You Need More

My daughter Pnina B. told me this "Only in Israel" story the other day. It happened to her a few weeks ago.

There were only a few days left before the summer ended, and Pnina very much wanted to go swimming at a beach.

Since her sister-in-law was going to a Tel Aviv separate-swimming beach the very next day with a group of religious women from the Old City of Jerusalem, Pnina decided to join them. So she reserved a place on the special chartered bus that the group had ordered, and everything seemed fine.

Pnina was particularly excited about going to a beach because she planned to take along her nine-month-old baby. He had never been to a beach before, and Pnina thought that he would probably love it. In addition to all of this, Pnina's sister-in-law would be bringing along several of her sisters, who would be happy to help baby-sit — which really made it sound great.

So everything was organized. As Pnina would be going straight from her place of work, it was arranged that the chartered bus would make a special stop at the exit to Jerusalem in order to pick up Pnina and the baby.

Fantastic.

Since Pnina works quite near to where she lives, and since her husband Ezriel was home from *kollel* that day, he brought the baby to Pnina shortly before she was to leave her place of employment.

So far, everything was going smoothly.

Upon arrival at Pnina's work-place, both she and Ezriel realized that it was silly for her to *shlep* the heavy baby carriage on a bus to the beach, and so her husband took the empty baby carriage back home with him, with the attached baby carriage bag, just leaving Pnina, the baby, and a plastic bag with some diapers in it.

Soon Pnina was finished at work, and was able to leave for the beach.

Seeing that it was later than she had expected, and that the bus she needed to take still hadn't come, and, being afraid that she might miss the special chartered bus if she waited too long, Pnina hailed a taxi-cab on the street. (Please note that this means that she had never used this cab driver before, and that the driver didn't know if she was a regular customer of his cab company or not.)

It didn't take the cab driver very long to get Pnina and the baby to the place where she was to meet the chartered bus.

However, as Pnina went for her wallet to pay the cab driver, she suddenly realized that she had left her wallet in the bag that was attached to the baby carriage. In other words, she had no money with her with which to pay the driver.

Explaining the whole story to the cab driver, Pnina asked this stranger if he would mind if she sent him the money the next day by mail, since she would miss the special bus if she went to her home with him now to get her wallet.

The driver, who had never seen her before in his life, agreed, and gave her his name and address so that she could send him the cab fare the next day.

Pnina thanked him profusely.

However, as Pnina opened the cab's door and started organizing herself and the baby to get out of the cab, the cab driver suddenly said, "Wait a minute. How are you going to pay the bus fare, and any other expenses at the beach?"

Truth to tell, Pnina hadn't thought of that, but she quickly responded, "Oh, *BeEzras HaShem* my sister-in-law will have extra money on her to lend me. She is supposed to be on the bus."

The cab driver wouldn't hear of it, and thrust 50 shekels at Pnina, saying, "Don't take a chance. Here's fifty shekels. You'll pay me back later."

Astounded wasn't the word for it. Here was a cab driver, a complete "stranger" who had never seen her before in his life, nor she, him, not only trusting her and lending her the original cab fare, but even worrying about her and the baby to the point of making sure that she would have enough money with her if anything came up at the beach!

After one or two attempts at reassuring the cab driver that she would be all right without his money-loan, Pnina finally accepted it with much gratitude. She then gave the cab driver *her* address, and told him to go to her home and tell her husband that she owed him money, and that he should pay him.

The cab driver asked if Ezriel would believe him, i.e., believe that Pnina had said to pay him 50 shekels plus the 25-shekel cab ride to the bus stop, and Pnina assured him that Ezriel would.

She then told the cab driver to turn on his meter as he drove to her house, so that her husband would be sure to pay him for this extra trip, too.

The cab driver was dumbfounded, and very appreciative that Pnina had thought of this, to the extent that he asked her, "Really? Are you sure it's okay if I do that?"

Of course, Pnina insisted that he do so. But what a country, and what a People! Amazing!

Baruch HaShem, Pnina made the chartered bus in time, and she got to the beach just fine, and the baby loved it, and, yes, she used the 50 shekels to take a cab home from the chartered bus's Jerusalem drop-off point.

And, yes, the cab driver got all of his money.

And Ezriel — well, he had a good chuckle, because he had realized that Pnina's wallet was in the baby's carriage bag, and so, with his typical thoroughness, he had taken the wallet out and put it into the plastic bag that Pnina was taking with her to the beach — the bag that held the baby's diapers!

What a marvelous country! And what an unusual, usual day.

Lost and Found

Edith F. is a prestigious Rebbetzin who lives in our neighborhood. She recently told me this story, which had happened to her not long ago. Really and truly, Only in Israel!

Rebbetzin F.'s husband had had a CAT scan done on his brain, and she had gone to the hospital to pick up the results. She traveled on the #27 bus since its bus-line runs very close to her home, and it stops right in front of the entrance to the hospital that she needed.

After getting the CAT scan's written results as well as the X-rays, Rebbetzin F.

boarded another #27 bus for her return trip home.

Though she was carrying the huge brown envelope which held both the X-rays and the results, she decided to get off the bus anyway for a quick "jump" into the out-door fresh food market of Machane Yehuda in order to pick up some fresh vegetables and a few fresh *pitot* [Middle Eastern-style bread], since the bus was passing right by the market. As the Rebbetzin had a monthly bus pass, it wouldn't cost any extra money to get on another bus.

After making her purchases, Rebbetzin F. returned to the bus stop, caught the next #27 bus, and then continued on her journey home.

However, upon walking into her apartment, she suddenly realized that she was no longer carrying the large brown envelope with her, the one that contained her husband's CAT scan results and X-rays.

Knowing how important they were, and how time-consuming and unpleasant it would be if her husband had to redo the CAT scan, Rebbetzin F. returned to Machane Yehuda in order to search for the large brown envelope.

Unfortunately, she couldn't find it there, and none of the vendors she had gone to had seen it either.

Returning home via another #27 bus, she told the bus driver what had happened and asked him for the phone number of the bus terminal at the end of the #27 line, thinking that perhaps she had inadvertently left the huge envelope on the original #27 bus, and that someone might have found it and therefore turned it in.

Sha'ar Shechem (Damascus Gate) was the #27 bus's terminal, and the driver gave her the phone number.

Upon Rebbetzin F.'s return home, she immediately phoned the number she had been given, and explained the entire story to the man who answered the phone. He checked his "lost-and-found" area and told her that, yes, she had left the CAT scan envelope on the bus, and that he had it.

Now, normally, when someone leaves something on a public bus, the person has to go down to that line's terminal and pick up the lost or forgotten item. Obviously. That only makes sense.

But I guess that the bus employee heard the tiredness in Rebbetzin F.'s voice. Or perhaps he just didn't want her to have to go through the inconvenience of *shlepping* around Sha'ar Shechem.

Because, when she asked him if he could please give the huge brown envelope to the next #27 bus driver coming up Shmuel HaNavi Street, which is where she lives, the bus employee immediately said that, yes, he would.

That in itself is amazing to me. (I do take it for granted, however, that items lost or forgotten on a bus will be turned in and collected at the bus's last stop, because I have lived here for over thirty years, and it happens all the time.)

Anyway, Rebbetzin F. went up to

Shmuel HaNavi Street, and waited for the next #27 bus to pass.

When it did, the driver asked if she was the woman who had lost an envelope. When she answered yes, he leaned over, and handed her the huge brown envelope with her husband's CAT scan results and X-rays inside.

Rebbetzin F. said "Thank you" to the bus driver, and he replied, "Glad I could help."

He then continued on his bus route.

What kindness and consideration! And what an unbelievable country and People.

Oh, Those Bus Trips!

What can I say? It seems like almost every bus ride here in Israel is a "happening" waiting to happen, as well as a possible learning and/or *mussar* experience. If you keep your eyes and ears open, that is.

Menachem D. works in the Givat Shaul neighborhood of Jerusalem. He takes the #11 bus, which is often crowded, to and from work.

One day the bus was particularly crowded, with people so packed in that they were literally pushed against the doors of the bus.

A soldier with a (folded) umbrella-type baby carriage squeezed onto the bus, holding what was obviously a very, very recently born baby.

A woman, who was standing inside the bus nearby, offered to hold the infant so that the soldier could pay the bus fare. (No, they didn't know each other.)

Problem was, that the bus was so packed, that people were constantly being pushed farther and farther back into the bus as everyone jostled to get into a position to either get off the bus or to take a soon-to-be-vacated seat.

And so the woman "stranger" who was holding the infant was gently pushed farther and farther away from the soldier holding the folded carriage, as he was still waiting to pay his bus fare.

Since that woman had to get off at the next bus stop, she gave the infant to a woman who was standing next to her to hold until the father could reclaim the baby.

But, almost immediately, this woman's

bus stop also approached, so of course she also passed the baby on to another woman standing behind her.

By this time, the infant was more than halfway back into the bus, and the soldier-father was still stuck at the front where he had boarded, unable to move farther back into the bus.

"We were packed in like sardines," commented Menachem as he told me what he had witnessed.

But this presented no problem for Israeli bus-travelers. When the most recent baby-holder needed to get off the bus, she too simply passed the baby on, giving it to another "stranger" to hold.

People kept getting off the bus at each stop (and passing the baby on from person to person), and the father was soon able to maneuver to the back of the bus to reclaim his infant.

However, as he approached the woman who was currently holding his baby, she got upset and held the infant even tighter.

"What? I just got the baby!" she complained. "Everyone on the bus has had a chance to hold this baby, and I don't? You'll just have to wait until I get off the bus."

So he did.

Luckily she reached her stop before he did!

Want a Ride?

This marvelous yet true story happened recently to the son of a friend of mine. His name is Aryeh W.

Aryeh is fifteen years old. Each day he comes home from Yeshiva during the lunch break. After lunch, he returns to his Yeshiva via bus.

Last week, though Aryeh thought he left home at the usual time, he saw his bus zoom past as he was walking to his stop.

Though Aryeh immediately began running as fast as he could in order to try and get to the bus stop before his bus would pull away from it, he didn't succeed, and missed the bus. Grinding to a halt, Aryeh stood on the sidewalk, watching as his bus drove away.

At that moment, a taxi-cab driver pulled up next to Aryeh and honked his horn.

The driver had seen Aryeh running after the bus, and he motioned to Aryeh to quickly get into his cab.

"Hurry and get in. I'll drive you to the next bus stop so that you can get your bus," offered the bareheaded cab driver whom Aryeh had never before seen in his life.

Aryeh thanked the man, but declined, saying that he didn't have the money to pay for a taxi-cab.

The driver shushed him, and told Aryeh to just quickly get into the cab; he wasn't talking about taking any money. He would just give him a ride to the next bus stop.

Appreciatively, Aryeh jumped into the cab and off they went, trying to catch up to the bus. (Please note that in many countries children will have been repeatedly warned never to get into a car with a stranger.

Baruch HaShem it still isn't like that in Israel, and so many various types of *chessed* can still flourish.)

To the chagrin of the fifteen-year-old boy and his cab driver, they reached the next bus stop only a few seconds after the bus had already pulled away.

Without a word, the driver again continued his race after Aryeh's bus, this time going quite a distance in order to reach the next bus stop on the line. (According to Israeli law, a bus driver can get a very large fine if he allows a passenger to get on or off his bus anywhere but at an officially designated bus stop.)

Looking out of his window, Aryeh saw a school friend of his who had also just missed the bus. Without thinking, Aryeh commented, "Oh, there's my friend Moishe."

The cab driver screeched to a halt and told Moishe to get in too, and then continued on his way.

This time the cab driver and his two

"passengers" got to the bus stop just as the bus was starting to pull away.

The cab driver began furiously honking his horn and waving his arm out of the window. He also cut off the bus by pulling up right in front of it, so that the bus wasn't able to go anywhere. Only then did he let out his two fare-free passengers at the bus stop.

What a nice *chessed* that Israeli cab driver did!

1) He allowed the two boys to get to their Yeshiva on time, and thus not miss any learning.

2) He gave Aryeh and his friend a free cab ride for quite a distance, since the two bus stops it took them to catch up to their bus were quite some distance from each other. And

3) He showed those two fifteen-year olds that every Jew, no matter how he is dressed, can appreciate the value of doing *chessed* and learning Torah.

What a good lesson it was for those two boys, and for everyone who hears this story.

And what an important lesson it was for me in how we should utilize everything that HaShem has given us for the benefit of others.

Though many times I am quick to do this with my "extra" time and with *maaser* money, I hope that I will always be as willing as that bareheaded cab driver to make use of the very tools of my livelihood to help another person, without asking for anything in return.

It is one thing to do someone you don't know a favor. But it is another thing to do the favor with the tools of your trade, for free.

I was very impressed when I heard this story, and proud that I live in a country where my children can see such behavior from many different types of people.

Tender Drivers

Bruchie C. made *aliya* to Israel with her large family about three or four years ago. Luckily for us, she moved into our neighborhood.

Bruchie is known as someone who is always willing, and happy, to do a *mitzva* wherever and whenever she is needed. She also encourages her children to be kind and helpful. And that makes this story, which Bruchie called to tell me, so nice....

As is to be expected, Bruchie's new *olim* children had to put in extra time with their schoolwork since even the boys, who had learned in Yeshivos in the United States, found that they were quite a bit behind in their fluency in Hebrew when it came to speaking and reading it all day long.

Which meant that "homework time" was particularly important and time-consuming.

As with many young *cheder* boys, Bruchie's first-grader (six years old) travels to and from *cheder* in a special *tender* [van] which gives door-to-door service.

This particular afternoon, when Bruchie's first-grader walked into their apartment, the first thing that Bruchie noticed was that her child was missing his *yalkut* [book-satchel].

After a few questions, the mystery was quickly solved. He had forgotten it on the *tender*, i.e., left it in the *cheder*'s van.

Though in America the chance of retrieving lost property was somewhat rare, even on a special school bus, Bruchie called the *tender* company's office anyway, to ask if by any chance they had seen her son's book-satchel.

The man in the office kept the phone

line with Bruchie open while he contacted
the van's driver via a two-way telephone, allowing Bruchie to overhear the conversation between the man in the office and the
driver of the van.

Within a minute, the driver confirmed
that, yes, the child's book-satchel was in his
van.

The man in the office asked the driver if
he could bring it right over to Bruchie.

The driver answered, "I've already finished my route" — i.e., I'm done for the day,
and want to go home.

The man in the office, however, who did
not know Bruchie or anyone else in her
family, immediately responded, "Go back
and bring her kid his homework, so he can
do it tonight."

Bruchie, overhearing this entire conversation, was in shock: she hadn't even mentioned the fact that she was fairly new to
Israel and therefore it was particularly important to her that her child keep up with his
homework each and every day.

Well, the van driver turned around from wherever in the city he was, and returned to Bruchie's neighborhood.

If fact, he even brought the book-satchel right up to her front door!

Tochacha Is Alive and Well in Israel

Yes, *tochacha*, rebuke and/or unsolicited advice, is alive and well in Israel today. You hear it from strangers on the street ("You should put a hat on your baby; the sun is strong today."), in the bank ("Why do you want to put this money in a savings plan today? Don't you know that the interest rates are supposed to go up tomorrow?"), and even from storekeepers ("Don't buy that shirt. It doesn't go with your suit.")

But *nothing* beats this bus driver story!

It happened a few months ago, on a Jerusalem bus. It was late afternoon, and the bus was packed with people.

You could tell that everyone was tired after a hard day of work/school/shopping, because there was little talking or laughing heard during the ride. The entire bus was particularly quiet, with everyone just calmly sitting or standing, waiting to get to their bus stop and to get home.

At each stop, several people got off the bus, and several people got on, so the bus remained full.

At a certain bus stop, a pregnant woman was one of the several people who boarded.

Perhaps everyone was so tired that they didn't notice her. Or perhaps everyone was so tired that they just decided to "skip it" this time.

But no one on the bus gave the pregnant woman a seat.

As the bus continued on its way, the bus driver noticed that the pregnant woman was still standing up, and had not been given a seat.

Bringing his bus to a halt on the side of the road, the bus driver stood up and said in a voice that was loud enough so that all of the passengers on the bus could hear: "*Please*, *Geveret* [Madam], take *my* seat."

I'm Not Taking Any Money from That Lady!

My friend Arlene H. is a *tzadekes*. The real, 100 percent *tzadekes* type who does *chessed* eighteen hours per day. When I mentioned this to her once, she commented, in all seriousness: "No, I don't do *chessed* eighteen hours every day. I don't do more than twelve, and on Friday I don't do any: I just prepare for Shabbos."

That is my friend Arlene.

And this is a true story that happened to my friend Arlene a few days ago....

One of the many types of kind deeds that Arlene does is helping poor families who need food: she collects money for them and pre-pays the butcher so that they can walk in like *mentschen* and just pick up "their" chickens, she leaves sums of money at the greengrocer so that other families can get especially nice fruits for Shabbos for their children, she periodically pays off a food bill in the *makolet* [a small neighborhood grocery store] for a family that is having a particularly hard time that month.

That's my friend Arlene.

Which is why I didn't even ask any questions about any of the details of this Only in Israel story she told me yesterday.

Arlene has a lot of contact with an organization called Yad Eliezer, which distributes food baskets to thousands of needy families each month. These are boxes filled with canned goods, bottles of oil, and other staples. All of these Yad Eliezer families are fine Jewish families which have been "checked out" extensively by Yad Eliezer before being added to their list of monthly recipients.

Since I know that Arlene often helps families to get on to the Yad Eliezer list, I was only mildly surprised when she told me that she was picking up the cartons of food, as she does every month, for two families who she knows cannot get the food boxes by themselves: Family X. has many, many small children and a "difficult husband" with emotional problems who will not and/or cannot get the food boxes, and Family Y. consists of a divorcee with serious health problems and her several small children, with no other family to help her carry the heavy boxes of food.

Since both families live very far from the Yad Eliezer food-distribution point, Arlene's son, who has a car, picks up the cartons of food with Arlene each month, and then delivers them to the homes of these two families, on the other side of town.

Last month Arlene's son had an important meeting and thus could only come hours after the food-distribution point closed. So Arlene decided she would go by herself to pick up the food, and her son would come to her home later that afternoon to pick up and then deliver the food packages.

But the cartons, filled with a month's supply of bottles of oil, packages of sugar and flour, and large-sized cans of olives, pickles, and various other food items, were too heavy for Arlene to carry. So she called a cab, and a nice man, a stranger walking past the food-distribution point, helped her *shlep* the heavy cartons to the curb.

Soon the cab arrived, complete with an undershirt-and-earring-wearing driver. Instead of *kvetching* about the large number of boxes, and/or demanding additional fare money for them which is the cab driver's legitimate right according to the law, the cab driver merely lugged the many, heavy cartons into his cab.

As they were speeding along, the cab driver asked Arlene why and where she was taking all of this food.

Arlene explained that the food was for two large families who didn't have husbands in the home who could pick up the food for them, and she told him a little about Yad Eliezer and the two families.

Upon arrival at her apartment complex, Arlene realized that she didn't have enough money to pay the cab driver, so she ran upstairs to her apartment to get more money. In the meantime, the cab driver expended quite a bit of effort unpacking the heavy food cartons from his cab.

To Arlene's surprise and delight, as she descended the steps in her apartment building, she saw that the cab driver had even lugged all of the heavy boxes into the entranceway of her apartment house, which is quite a distance from the curb.

However, when she returned to the street where the cab had been parked so that she could pay and thank the driver, neither the cab nor the cab driver were anywhere to be seen.

Arlene returned to her home and immediately called the cab company. (No, there was no fear in leaving the food cartons downstairs in the building's lobby until her son would arrive.)

Arlene gave the taxi-cab dispatcher her address and explained that the cab she had taken had left without her having paid the driver.

On the phone Arlene overheard the dispatcher contact her cab driver, and then say to him: "Yaacov, the lady says that you forgot to get your cab-fare money from her."

Still on the open line, Arlene also overheard what the cab driver's response to the dispatcher was; the cab driver, who had never seen Arlene before in his life, and who had never previously heard of Yad Eliezer nor of all of the *chessed* that they do.

Over the phone, Arlene heard her cab driver say to the dispatcher: "*I'm* not taking any money from *that* lady! Tell her to give it to *tzedaka*."

Perspectives on Irritations

Yes, it is true. Irritating, upsetting, aggravating, even infuriating things happen everywhere in the world.

And, yes, Israel is no exception. Such things do happen to a person here, too.

However, I think that, if you can look at the source of your irritation from different angles, you might be able to see the irritation in a different light. Especially since, here in Israel, the response sometimes elicited from people around you is different from what you'd expect.

Take, for example, what happened to

my friend Dossi L.

Dossi lives in the Ramot neighborhood of Jerusalem, and travels to and from the main city center several times a week by bus.

She called me the other day to tell me what she personally overheard....

It was a week-day, in the early afternoon, when many people finish their day's work and the stores are closing. My friend Dossi had been in the city and was waiting at her bus stop for the bus to Ramot in order to return home.

Usually the bus comes every six to nine minutes, but for some reason it was late that day.

The number of people standing and waiting for the bus kept increasing as more and more people came to the bus stop; but no buses arrived to take the people away.

After a while Dossi noticed a woman who was holding a baby. This woman seemed particularly upset that the bus had still not arrived. In fact, though many of the people were muttering to themselves and asking each other why the bus still hadn't come (as if anyone could possibly know — but that is Israel!), this woman stood out.

She was upset almost to distraction.

Soon a Ramot bus that looked only half-full passed by without stopping. (In truth, the bus only had the *appearance* of being half-full of passengers, because, from the sidewalk, a person can never *really* be sure of what is truly going on inside the bus. But, standing and waiting on the sidewalk, it sure is infuriating to watch the bus as it passes by.)

By this time, the woman holding the baby was almost in tears. Though she and Dossi had never met nor even seen each other before, the woman proceeded to explain to Dossi that she had been waiting for almost half an hour for the bus, and that she really had to get home.

It was at this point that the next bus to Ramot came.

Several people who boarded the bus muttered to the driver and/or commented out loud about the fact that they had been forced to wait for the bus an inordinately long period of time.

Dossi was among the first group of people boarding the bus, and so she overheard what the bus driver answered the woman who was carrying the baby.

As the baby-carrying lady was paying her bus fare, she also complained to the driver about the fact that everyone had had to wait so long and that a half-empty bus had then driven by without stopping, forcing everyone to have to wait even longer for another bus.

The driver, who was not wearing a *kippa*, answered the woman very directly.

"*Geveret*," he responded, "*hakol b'yedey Shamayim, chutz mi-yiras Shamayim.*" ["Everything is in the hands of Heaven, except for fear of Heaven."]

Go fight that.

It's never easy raising a family. And it is even harder when you are doing the raising all by yourself. But, time and time again, HaShem shows us that, especially in Israel, you are never really all on your own.

Costs Less by Bus

My friend Faigie F. got divorced several years ago, and therefore is raising her five children all by herself here in Jerusalem. Her eldest son is presently learning and boarding at a Yeshiva near Tel Aviv. Since the pre-divorce years were as difficult as the actual divorce years, if not even more so, this child was particularly affected by all of the rancor and disillusionment.

And, the fact that he is now a teenager isn't making it any easier, as you can imagine.

Being a very good and responsible mother, Faigie arranged for several counseling sessions for her rebellious teen. Since the health care system subsidizes these counseling sessions, they take place in the municipality in which the family lives, as would be expected.

A few weeks ago, Faigie's son had a Friday morning appointment, and so he came into Jerusalem for the morning.

However, instead of going straight home after the early-morning counseling session, or returning directly to his Yeshiva, son #1 didn't do either. In fact, he didn't show up at his home until almost 1:30 in the afternoon (Shabbos was after 4:00 P.M.).

Knowing that, for this child in particular, it was important that he not "cut" Yeshiva but rather return there in time for Shabbos, a very tense Faigie called and ordered him a "special" (i.e., a regular, private taxi-cab), to take him all the way to his Yeshiva. Though Faigie is always on a tight budget, this, she knew, was important, as it was already too late for him to return to Yeshiva by bus (he would have needed to take a few) or to take a *sherut* [a cheap taxi, shared by several people, which only leaves after all the places are taken].

So she ordered him a private taxi-cab.

In only a few minutes the cab driver arrived, complete with a ponytail.

As Faigie put her son into the taxi-cab, she very strongly told the driver, "Take him straight to this address. Do not let him talk you into going anywhere else. Do not go to the right nor to the left. Only straight and directly to the Yeshiva."

The ponytailed taxi driver understood, and answered, "I'll take him right there, and I'll talk to him."

Then, turning to his young passenger, the driver asked, "Why are you making trouble for your mother? Where were you all day that you are leaving for the Yeshiva so late? Do you know how expensive a private taxi-cab is to Tel Aviv?"

The driver then turned to an astonished Faigie and asked her, "Are you sure that you want to send him by private cab and not keep him home until after Shabbos so that you can send him back *motzaei Shabbos* by bus? He deserves having to *shlep* back by bus. And it will cost you a lot less money."

Yes, this is really what happened. I even rechecked the dialogue with Faigie after I wrote it down!

And, yes, the cab driver did actually give Faigie's son a "talking to" during their inter-city ride. (And, yes, he surely got back in time for Shabbos, too.)

What a truly unbelievable country, and what a truly unbelievably *unbelievable* People!

Part II:
Shopkeepers

It's Cheaper Over There

Our small neighborhood felafel store has a "charge it" plan for those people who buy felafel there often.

What is a "charge it" plan for a small, neighborhood business in Israel? They simply write down your name and the amount of money that you owe them in a small, cheap notebook.

Since my friend Channie P. often buys felafel in that felafel store, she has a "charge account" there. They also sell a type of whipped ice cream from a special machine, which Channie had never tried.

One *motzaei Shabbos*, her (large) family and (many) guests wanted some ice cream. Knowing that the felafel store opens *motzaei Shabbos*, and that they sell this whipped ice cream, Channie ran out of her house — without taking any money with her — in order to purchase it there.

However, when the felafel man told Channie how expensive her order would be, she balked. She hadn't realized that this whipped ice cream would be so much more expensive than regular ice cream. And she was buying for a lot of people.

Seeing the expression on Channie's face, the felafel man said to her, "Go over to the nut store next door. They also sell ice cream, but the regular kind. The ice cream will be cheaper over there."

So, thanking the felafel man, Channie went next door to buy the other ice cream.

The felafel man had been correct: the ice cream in the nut store was only 14 shekels for an entire package, much cheaper than the whipped ice cream that the felafel man was selling. Except that, at this point, Channie suddenly remembered that she didn't have any money with her — and she didn't feel like going all the way home to get her wallet.

So, Only in Israel, Channie went back to the felafel store, and told the owner, "You were right. The ice cream is cheaper over there. I know this is *chutzpa*, but, since I didn't bring any money with me and I'd rather not have to return home in order to get some, would you give me the amount I need, and charge it to my bill?"

The felafel man answered, "*Ayn baaya* [no problem]," and gave her the money that she needed so that she could *buy a product which he also sold*, even though she was buying it, cheaper, at a nearby competitor.

As Channie finished telling me this amazing "daily life situation in Israel" story, she suddenly stopped and exclaimed, "My goodness! That I would even *think* to ask a store owner such a thing! Really — Only in Israel!"

Shopping in Israel

Kindness and consideration exist everywhere, to be sure. But somehow, when it has to do with stores and businesses, one is a little more surprised to see these qualities.

My friend Sarah W. had gone grocery shopping for her large family at a distant supermarket one morning. Since she had made quite an extensive order, she assumed that the store would deliver the order to her home, hopefully free of charge.

Yes, they agreed to deliver her food order for free, but they asked her what time she would be at home.

She told them, and then left the store.

Unfortunately, after Sarah got home, something came up and she forgot all about her food delivery, and her commitment to be at home for it. She just left her house, with no one at home, and went about her business.

Upon returning home several hours later, Sarah found that her food delivery had arrived. Piled high in front of her door were all of the cans and boxes that she had bought, everything stacked neatly in a small mountain of food.

While putting the food away once inside her home, Sarah suddenly realized that none of the meat products that she had purchased were to be found. Since all of the other food items were present and accounted for, Sarah started wondering if perhaps they had been forgotten by the store, or, though very hard to believe, perhaps they had somehow been taken from in front of her door while she wasn't home.

As Sarah was pondering this dilemma, the doorbell rang.

There stood the deliveryman, holding Sarah's bags of meat.

"You weren't home when we delivered your food order," the man explained, "so we didn't leave your meat. We were afraid that it might spoil while you were gone, or that perhaps cats or bugs might get to it. So we took it back to the store, and thought that we'd try to deliver it again later. Glad you're home — here is your meat."

That the deliverymen put such thought and consideration into their work was very gratifying to Sarah. But that they didn't even charge her for the extra, additional home delivery, which was completely her own fault since she *had* told them that she would be at home and then she wasn't, was really going way beyond being kind.

But that is Israel, and the Israelis....

Another time Sarah called to tell me that she had just returned from shopping in a very large, new *Charedi* supermarket that had recently opened. [What is a "*Charedi* supermarket," you ask? Unlike regular Israeli supermarkets which sell both kosher and *kosher le'mehadrin* products, *Charedi* supermarkets sell food items that are exclusively *mehadrin*.]

What did Sarah have to report on after her shopping spree?

While going up and down the aisles, Sarah heard the supermarket's loudspeaker system periodically announcing "Best Buys," and various items that were on sale throughout the store.

Suddenly, the loudspeaker's authoritarian voice came booming out again — this time announcing that a *minyan* for *mincha* was forming in a back room of the supermarket, for anyone who hadn't *davened* yet.

Grocery shopping in Eretz Yisroel.

From a Simple Haircut...

Aliza K. has only been in Israel for a year or two. She had been touring Europe with some friends after having finished graduate school, but then, "suddenly," she decided to come over to see Israel as well.

Parting ways with her friends, Aliza arrived in Israel and found herself in love with the Land of Israel and with its people. It also didn't take her long to become enthralled with the new view of Judaism to which she was exposed for the first time.

Soon Aliza was studying about her Heritage part-time at a girls' seminary for *baalos teshuva* in Jerusalem.

One day a fellow student asked Aliza to accompany her to a downtown beauty salon where she was going in order to get a haircut.

Being free that afternoon, Aliza readily agreed.

Hurrying to the hair appointment through the afternoon crowd of people jamming the busy downtown Jerusalem streets, Aliza was touched, as always, by the wonder of the Jews' return to their Land in modern times. And by her personal joy in being a part of it.

After waiting some time for the hair stylist to finish with a previous client and start working on her friend, Aliza suddenly realized that she needed to *daven mincha*, and though she had a *Tehillim* with her, she did not have a *siddur*. The beauty parlor didn't have one anywhere either.

But, Israel being Israel, Aliza knew that almost every two or three Jerusalem streets has a little *shul* hidden somewhere on it, even in the downtown, commercial area of the city.

So, out she went to explore the downtown area.

Aliza reached Rehov Yaffo, one of Jerusalem's main streets, and began walking towards a small *Beis Midrash* that she remembered being down the street and to the right.

As she walked, she passed a small "hole-in-the-wall" kiosk [a very small store selling cigarettes, candy, and drinks].

Suddenly the owner called out to her, "*Geveret*, come over here one minute, please."

Though in a hurry, Aliza complied. And got the surprise of her life.

"Will you watch my kiosk for me a while, while I run to *daven mincha* with a *minyan*?" the owner of the kiosk asked her.

Aliza answered in a calm, normal voice, without even thinking about the fact that a stranger was asking her, a complete stranger, to watch his store for him.

"Do you mind if I say *Tehillim* while I do it?" she asked.

"No," was the reply.

So, figuring that the man had a special obligation to *daven* with a *minyan*, and that she could *daven mincha* later without one, Aliza squeezed behind the counter to watch this man's store for him.

As she was reciting *Tehillim*, people periodically came up to the kiosk and, without saying anything to her, just took the various items that they wanted, leaving the exact change behind on the counter. Aliza was relieved about that, since she didn't know the prices of anything.

But it was amazing to her to see that people kept coming and going, taking items from the kiosk, and leaving the correct change on the counter, as she sat there, saying *Tehillim* and looking up expectantly each time someone stopped by. These obviously were regular customers, who knew the prices of the items they were buying, and who didn't seem at all surprised to see a stranger sitting there, saying *Tehillim*, and only looking up when necessary.

About twenty minutes later the kiosk owner returned, thanking her profusely.

As Aliza continued her walk to the little *Beis Midrash* to get a *siddur* from which she could *daven mincha*, she marveled at the *mitzva* she had just gotten, and at the unbelievableness of a stranger leaving his entire store, including all of its contents, as well as his cash box full of money, in the hands of a complete stranger, so that he could go and *daven* with a *minyan*.

And she marveled at the fact that the reason she was chosen to help him from the many people hurrying past the kiosk was, probably, because she was dressed in a very modest manner. And so the kiosk owner probably figured that she was trustworthy.

How amazing.

The country, the People, and our unbelievably beautiful Heritage.

Have a Special Day

My friend Dafna M. called me the other day to tell me about an unusual, "usual" situation she had heard about from a friend at work.

A couple living in Jerusalem wanted to celebrate their anniversary by doing something special. Being the parents of many, many children, they didn't want it to cost a lot of money, though they still wanted to somehow spend a quiet, relaxed, elegant evening together.

Finally they came up with the perfect solution: they would go to a fancy five-star hotel in Jerusalem, and have coffee.

Perfect. Quiet. Beautiful. Elegant. And two cups of coffee, they could afford.

Sitting there sipping their coffee, a mutual friend walked by, and asked what they were doing there. After being told the story, and offering a hearty *mazal tov* for their anniversary, he continued on to pay his bill.

In Israel, it is not unusual to chat with the cashier while he or she is fiddling with the customer's charge card. So, while the friend waited to sign his charge card form, he mentioned to the cashier that the couple on the left was celebrating their anniversary by having coffee at the hotel.

As a joke, he threw out, "Can't you do something for them, since they can't afford anything else in this hotel?"

Well, the friend took back his charge card and signed the form, said good-by, and left... and only found out later what had happened because of his "joke."

The cashier spoke to a waiter, who spoke to the *maitre d'*, who told the waitress to bring the couple a complimentary ice cream Sundae Supreme in honor of their anniversary.

Needless to say, the couple was speechless when the waitress appeared at their table with a huge sundae for two, complete with two sparklers, little umbrellas, and lots of ice cream in various colors, all "on the house."

I was impressed by this story, but not shocked. Because five years earlier I had taken my eighteen-year-old daughter for a special birthday-present trip to Haifa where we stayed overnight in the most beautiful and most luxurious hotel in the city. It was also the most expensive, but I knew my daughter (and I) would really enjoy and appreciate this special treat.

When making our reservations by telephone, I explained to the Hotel's reception/booking clerk that I wanted to be sure that we got one of the nicest rooms, with a view overlooking the sea, even if it cost extra money. During our conversation I explained that, since we lived here and weren't tourists, this might be the only time my daughter would ever get to stay in such a beautiful, luxurious hotel, and that we were only coming since it was a special birthday for her.

Fine. I made the reservation. And the clerk assured me that she would assign us a really special room.

We arrived in Haifa, checked in, and went upstairs to the room. The booking clerk had really outdone herself. We had been given one of the few rooms that the hotel holds for important dignitaries. It was really special. And, in addition to the fantastic room, on the bureau was a gorgeous, unbelievably huge, nut cake, with a "Happy Birthday, Compliments of the Haifa X Hotel" card attached.

Please note: they hadn't given us one or two pieces of cake, nor even several large pieces, which would have been nice, and impressive, enough. What they had done was to give us, without charge, a huge, gigantic part of a sheet cake, big enough for at least thirty people! And, to make this action even more unbelievable, they could not even have hoped for any advertising/public relations value from it, since they knew that we would probably never be returning for another stay!!

What a special country, and what a special People!

Take What You Want

My friend Ruth G. was out shopping the other day, and, among other things, she also needed some ribbons, buttons, and other sundry sewing items. Since she was already in the Jerusalem neighborhood of Geula, she went into a sewing/notions store that she knew about, which was nearby.

Now, please note, if you didn't know that this "store" existed, you would never, ever just bump into it. It's, well, near Kikar Shabbos, just at the back of a very, *very* small alley.

Kitchen chairs of various descriptions

are laid out and piled up in front of the entrance to this narrow alley, and so it is only by walking between these chairs that a person can reach and enter the alley itself.

This (really tiny) alley is flanked, on both sides, with all types and sizes of chairs. A couch, piled on top of another couch, lines part of the left wall. Between two dining room chairs on the right side of the wall there is a door that leads into the sewing store.

It appears that this "furniture store" and the sewing store both belong to the same family, a husband and wife team. The chair-sofa store, run by a small Sephardic man who seems to be constantly sitting on one of his chairs saying *Tehillim*, opens around 9:00 or 9:30 A.M. The sewing store is supposed to open around 10:00 A.M.

On this particular day that Ruth went to the sewing store, it was closed. Undaunted, she returned later, but all was still dark inside, and the door to the store was still closed.

This time, however, the owner of the "furniture store" looked up from his *sefer* and said to Ruth, "Go right in and turn on the light. Take what you want, and give me the money."

Ruth was pleasantly surprised, and since she did need those ribbons and buttons, she opened the (unlocked) door to the dark store, and searched for the light switch (which she soon found).

Turning it on, she began roaming around in the two rooms of the notions store, comparing colors of the myriad rolls of ribbons adorning the walls, and opening and closing little doors to the many different button-drawers.

The little man was nowhere in sight.

Picking out the buttons she wanted, Ruth jotted down the price of each button on a little piece of paper she found in her purse. She knew what the prices of the various buttons were because each individual price was written on the front of each little plastic button-drawer.

Scrounging around, Ruth found the scissors, and proceeded to measure out the different ribbons against the measuring stick that was attached to the counter. Here again, the price per meter of each of the different types of ribbon was written on the spool, and she thus did some quick calculations and added together the entire amount.

Proud of herself and of her accomplishments — Ruth had never measured and "professionally cut" ribbon before — she counted out the exact amount which she owed the owners, turned off the lights and closed the door, and went outside to make an accounting to the "furniture-store" man.

Looking up from his *Tehillim*, he accepted her money *and never even asked what she had taken.* Nor did he ask to see the accounting she had made!

Ruth was astounded, and called me soon after she returned home from her outing.

"I'm not even a regular customer there,"

Ruth exclaimed. "The man doesn't know me at all! And I must have been wandering about in the empty store, all alone, for at least twenty minutes! Can you believe it?!"

What a truly unbelievable country and People!

And, as I write these lines, I suddenly realized that there was also an unlocked cash register on the counter in the store (I've been in there) ... yet neither Ruth nor I even thought about mentioning that fact when the story was related to me!

What can you say?!

A Quick Minyan

This true story goes to show how easy it can be to *daven* with a *minyan* in Eretz Yisroel. How very, very easy, and convenient.

My friend Leslie R. was shopping in the Geula neighborhood of Jerusalem when she remembered that she had to buy some film.

Walking into the Geula film store, there were only one or two people in line in front of her.

A blond *Chassid* and his brother were working in the film store, obviously the owners. Within seconds the people in front of Leslie were taken care of and had left the store. Leslie, meanwhile, was looking at some pretty picture albums, considering if perhaps she would buy a few in addition to the film she needed.

Suddenly the voice of the blond *Chassid* interrupted Leslie's musings. In a kind and gentle manner, he asked her if she would please hurry and decide what she wanted to buy.

The reason the store owner gave for rushing his customer? "It is now ten minutes to five. I have a *minyan* in five minutes," he said.

Leslie, unruffled, bought the film she needed, paid, and left the store.

As she was walking out, at five minutes to five, she noticed several men walking towards the film store.

They went in.

Curious, Leslie watched, and counted, as men filed passed her and went into the film store singly and in pairs.

At five o'clock, when Leslie walked away, she had counted over twenty men going into that film store.

Leslie was amazed, and delighted. How convenient for the store owners who worked nearby — they just had to close their own stores for a few minutes and walk a few doors down from their own stores to *daven*!

And what an unbelievable *chessed* to do for all the men in the neighborhood, and for passersby, having a *minyan* in a store right in the middle of a busy street.

And what an unbelievable way to run a business!

Contact Chessed

Anna W. (now Anna Y.) woke up on the morning of her wedding nervous, happy, and excited.

Since Anna was the first child in her family to get married, her parents shared her emotions completely. Truly a happy, exciting, and momentous day. With lots and lots of last-minute things to do — no matter how organized and prepared they had thought they would be.

Suddenly, in the middle of the flurry of activity, Anna realized that she was missing something — one of her contact lenses. And it was nowhere to be found. Absolutely nowhere.

Anna had worn contact lenses for many years, and most certainly did not want to appear in public now, on her wedding day, in glasses — particularly as she would then be engraved in the minds of everyone that way, for eternity, wearing glasses, in hundreds of wedding photographs!

In fact, Anna didn't even think that she still *owned* a pair of glasses anymore with her correct prescription.

What to do? She certainly couldn't attend her own wedding unable to see anybody or anything!

Despite the fact that everyone in the family knew that it takes several days to order and get new contact lenses, Anna's father called the optometrist that the family used, anyway.

Anna's father began explaining the situation to the optometrist, hoping that in some way, somehow, he could convince the man to make Anna another pair of lenses that very day. [Note: at that time, contact lenses were only made and sold in pairs, never individually.]

"I know that it usually takes a few days to get contact lenses," Anna's father implored the optometrist, "but it would be so very, *very* kind of you if somehow you would do this for us. Please, my daughter is getting married today. I know it is unheard of to get same-day service, but I'll pay you any amount of money that you want to charge us. Any amount at all. Please! We'll do anything. She really needs those lenses!"

"What?!" the optometrist responded. "She's getting married today? Don't worry. I'll make you only one lens. It will be ready in a few hours. And there is no charge. No charge at all. *Mazal tov, mazal tov*!"

So Anna was married that day, wearing contact lenses. And she, and her wedding pictures, were truly beautiful.

Nine Shekels' Worth

Some daily-life experiences are big and momentous. Others are seemingly small and inconsequential. But somehow, in Israel, no daily-life experience is insignificant.

My son-in-law's brother-in-law, Pinchas G., told us about this "little thing" a few weeks ago....

Several years ago a small, fresh-squeezed juice stand opened in the Geula neighborhood of Jerusalem. By small, I mean that there is a counter, a carrot juicer, a squeezer that makes fresh orange or grapefruit juice, a blender, a napkin holder, and a cash register — and space for one person to squeeze by.

Pinchas, who teaches nearby, goes there every day for a glass of freshly squeezed juice. Every Sunday through Friday, he buys the medium-sized glass, which currently costs nine shekels (approximately $2 [1.3 ₤]). The smaller-sized glass of freshly squeezed juice costs eight shekels, and the largest-sized glass costs ten shekels.

But there is one small complication. Pinchas likes his juice very, very cold.

When he first started going to this small fresh-juice stand, he used to always ask the man behind the counter to put a lot of ice into his glass. Each of the two men working there had a different system for doing this. (Pinchas has since realized that one of the men is the owner of the juice stand, and the other man is his employee.)

Without ever a word or a sign of any type from Pinchas that he expects anything other then some ice added into his nine-shekel glass of juice, the employee, when he is there, invariably gives Pinchas a nine-shekel glass of juice, tells him to drink a little bit of it, and then asks for the glass back. The employee then adds ice to Pinchas' nine-shekel glass of juice.

When the owner of the juice stand is working, on the other hand, he has a different system to ensure that Pinchas is getting his full nine-shekels' worth of juice. The owner fills up a nine-shekel-sized glass with the fresh juice, then pours the whole thing into a ten-shekel-sized glass. Only then does the owner add the ice, to the larger glass.

With the passage of time, Pinchas has become a steady customer. Which means that, by now, he doesn't even have to ask for ice. Both the owner of the juice stand as well as his employee recognize and remember that Pinchas likes his juice very cold.

So now, when Pinchas comes into the store, both owner and employee automatically give him his juice with a lot of ice, though each worker uses his own system to ensure that Pinchas is given his money's worth of juice. Pinchas is always amazed how both put kindness and honesty (beyond the letter of the law) before profit, for neither is obligated to subsidize his desire for ice.

At superficial glance these are just average people, doing small things in their everyday life. But, even if these acts appear to be small, they most certainly are not inconsequential. I pray that I will always be as careful with money matters and all questions of honesty, as those two men are.

What a People, and what a country!

Don't Judge a Book by Its Cover

Sometimes things in Israel are not just cute or nice, but also surprisingly interesting in concept. My friend Sheri C. had an example of just such an interestingly unexpected experience when she first made *aliya* around six years ago.

It was the summertime, and particularly hot.

Sheri and her family had just arrived a few days earlier from Brooklyn, New York, where she had sold a large three-story house. Most of their belongings, and all of their household furnishings, had been shipped to Israel, so, being a large family on a restricted budget, they had rented an un-furnished apartment.

Trouble was, their lift of belongings had not yet cleared through customs, and so their unfurnished apartment was unfur-nished. And Sheri had six children. And she was pregnant. And new in the country. And it was very, very hot.

The children had no problems — they were all outside, playing, happily making new friends. But Sheri was boilingly hot.

Suddenly she noticed that her entire (huge) *mirpeset* [outdoor balcony] was filled, literally crawling, with tiny black bugs. Soon they were swarming everywhere, in-side and out.

After screaming, she got the name of an exterminator, and called him. He came im-mediately.

Now, being from the States, Sheri was used to pregnant women staying far, far away from any spraying exterminator. But this Jewish exterminator seemed to have another, different type of spray and system of spraying, because, as he was spraying every inch of Sheri's porch and apartment, he kept up a sprightly conversation with her.

Truth to tell, being *very* new to Israel, Sheri was a little awed by the fact that her exterminator was Jewish, and speaking Hebrew. In fact, everything was very new, and amazing, to her, though this bug experience was certainly less than pleasant. But the man did seem like a very good exterminator.

Finally he finished spraying everywhere, and packed up his things.

As he was leaving, he suddenly turned and said, "Oh, I have something for you."

Expecting a business card with his phone number, or pehaps a magnet for her refrigerator advertising his services, Sheri was shocked to be handed a small *sefer Tehillim*.

And what do you think the connection was between the exterminator and his handing out copies of a small *sefer Tehillim* to his customers?

You probably guessed it, though it took Sheri a few minutes to believe it.

In tastefully designed lettering, on the cover of the *Tehillim*, his exterminating advertisement was to be found, complete with his phone number and the slogan, "We will kill your bugs...."

Truly, Only in Israel.

And truly the best way of keeping unpleasant things away!

Part III:
"Strangers"

I Was Waiting for You

This is a true story that happened to me many years ago, but it is a story that I will never forget. Because of what happened, I now have a "thing" about locking front doors, though, truth to tell, even before this I was always careful about making sure that doors were locked. After all, one never knows....

We had been living in our Jerusalem apartment for approximately two years. My husband and I had an appointment one evening, on a *motzaei Shabbos*, and we were hurrying to leave our apartment, and to get to our destination on time.

As we stepped into the elevator of our apartment building, I asked my husband, as I always did three or four times, if we had locked the front door of our apartment. Knowing that we always do, he answered in the affirmative.

Being innately careful about the need to lock doors, as our elevator descended I again repeated my query of whether or not our front door was locked.

Yes, he assured me. Nothing to worry about. The front door was locked.

Fine....

Quite a few hours later we returned home.

I don't know what made me try the front door handle before putting my key into the lock, but I did.

The door was unlocked.

We charily pushed open the front door, and walked in.

Facing us, sitting at the head of our very large, heavy mahogany dining-room table, next to our full-of-silver silver-cabinet, sat a huge *Chassid*.

A very big man, he was wearing a large *shtreimel* and was dressed in a long black coat.

As we walked into the room, this large stranger smiled and said, "I came to collect *tzedaka* money for a needy bride. Your door was open, but no one was home. I was afraid to leave your door unlocked, so I waited until you returned."

At which point he got up, and walked out.

We were so shocked to see this huge stranger sitting at our dining room table that till today we do not remember whether or not we gave him any *tzedaka* money — or any money for the hours he had spent as a *shomer*, guarding our home and thus not being able to go around collecting the *tzedaka* money for which he had come.

But one thing I do know: only in Israel could a stranger spend his entire evening babysitting a stranger's house so that no dishonest strangers should enter it.

Money

Maybe I'm wrong, but it seems to me that the attitude of many people in Israel towards money is very different from that espoused by most people in other countries.

For example: Devora E., the eight-year-old granddaughter of my neighbor Mrs. P., recounted this "observed-while-traveling-on-the-bus" story to her grandmother, who then told it to me.

Devora was coming home from school by bus, as usual. However, this day, there was a little girl on the bus who was traveling alone, and who had fallen asleep on the bus.

Suddenly the little girl woke up, looked

around, and started crying. It seems that she realized she had missed her bus stop, and so she just sat there, crying.

A woman who was sitting nearby asked the child what was wrong. The little girl proceeded to explain that she had gone past the bus stop at which she needed to get off.

As the bus sped along, this woman stranger reassured the little girl, "It's all right. Stop crying. Everything will be fine. Here is the money for another bus ride. Get off this bus at the next stop, cross the street, and take the bus back to where you should have gotten off."

At the next red light the bus driver, who had overheard the entire conversation, turned around in his seat and said to the woman, "Here, take half the fare money from me. I *also* want a share in this *mitzva*."

And he gave the woman stranger half the bus-fare money.

Comments: 1) No, the bus driver was not wearing a *kippa*, and

2) Can you imagine the *chinuch* lesson

this provided for an eight-year-old child observer on a regular, everyday bus ride?

Then there is the story of Malka F., who called me up especially to tell me about what had happened to her husband recently.

It seems that every few months, Malka and her husband go out to dinner with some friends, another couple they know well.

As they all go out together regularly, they have developed a system whereby, alternately, one couple pays for the meal, and the other couple leaves the tip. The next time they meet, the payers and tippers switch roles.

This particular evening, the couples went to a Jerusalem restaurant called Off the Square. But when Malka and her husband returned home after a lovely dinner, they suddenly realized that, though this time the other couple had paid for the meal, they had forgotten to leave the tip.

Calling the restaurant, Malka's husband explained to the owner that they had just eaten there, but that he had forgotten to leave a tip. He asked that the owner please explain this to the waiter, and that he tell him that, although he couldn't come in this week, he would try to come in the next week in order to pay the waiter his tip.

Only in Israel would the restaurant owner respond by telling Malka's husband that *he* would lay out the money for him, and that he could reimburse him later. He then asked Malka's husband, whom he didn't know, how much money he wanted to leave as a tip for the waiter.

The Remarkable "Stranger"

Risa L. spent last Shabbos at the home of my friend Shifra S. It was there that she saw, and read, ON BUS DRIVERS, DREIDELS AND ORANGE JUICE, a collection of true stories about life in Israel.

After putting the book down, Risa turned to Shifra and said, "I have a story that happened to me a few months ago that is even more unbelievable than these!"

And she proceeded to relate what happened to her on her way back to the Neve Yerushalayim dorm one night....

Risa had already been in Israel for over

six months. During that time she had "dis-
covered" her Jewish Heritage and "found"
Neve Yerushalayim, a *baalas teshuva* seminary for girls in the Har Nof neighborhood of
Jerusalem. She studied hard and was learning a lot. And, periodically, she went to the
Kosel after her evening classes were over,
to say *Tehillim.*

This night was no different from any
other night as Risa traveled the fifty-minute
bus ride to the *Kosel* — except that she
stayed longer than usual at the *Kosel*, and
only just made the last bus back to Har Nof.

Since Risa was very tired, and since Har
Nof was at the opposite end of the #2
bus-line from where she had boarded, Risa
unwittingly fell asleep in the dark, quiet,
fairly empty bus.

Now, please remember that Risa was
still relatively new to Jerusalem in general,
and to Har Nof in particular. So, when she
woke up with a start as the bus stopped and
the driver told her that this was the last stop,
she was a trifle confused when she got off.

By the time the bus had left the area and Risa had collected herself enough to look around in the darkness, she realized that she had no idea where in Har Nof she was.

The street was very, very dark, and it was also very, very empty of any movement.

Suddenly, in the darkness, Risa noticed a man walking towards a nearby house.

Though it was by now after midnight, and the area was completely desolate, Risa approached the stranger and asked him in which direction she should walk in order to get to the Neve Yerushalayim campus.

The man immediately answered, "I'll take you: it is too far for you to walk." He then entered his house, presumably to get his car keys.

Risa stood on the lonely, dark pavement, wondering what her mother would think of her daughter, in the middle of the night, going up to talk to a complete stranger — and a man at that! — and then willingly taking a ride with him in a car!

At that point, the front door opened, and

the man's wife came out, holding the car keys.

As she drove Risa to the Neve Yerushalayim dorm, this "stranger" invited Risa for a Shabbos meal. When Risa thanked her, but replied that she already was invited somewhere, the woman asked if Risa had any family in Israel.

"No. No one," answered Risa.

At which point this stranger, wife of a stranger, this never-before-seen, unknown Har Nof resident, replied, "Well, you do now. Us. Come to us whenever you want."

Life in Israel. One big family.

With its problems and some disappointments, perhaps, but still, one People. One family.

I Know It's Everywhere, but...

I know that people are honest everywhere, and that it is the person and not the place that makes one honest or not, but I just can't get over the amazement my friend Helene S. displayed when she told me what she had experienced on a Jerusalem bus, shortly after she and her husband and children had made *aliya* from Flatbush, New York.

We had been talking about how amazing it is to travel by bus, and I commented that, if you go by car, you miss out on seeing many of the beautiful situations that help make life in Israel so special.

Helene agreed, and told me how impressed she was the first time she had seen people passing money up and down the aisles in a crowded bus.

She was traveling back to her apartment after buying some vegetables at the Machane Yehuda *shuk*. The bus was filling up with people, all *shlepping* their many heavy packages onto the bus.

Soon the bus became packed with people and their bags of fresh fruits and vegetables. (Note: *every* day the bus becomes packed with people and their fruits and vegetables at Machane Yehuda market. The sheer abundance of fresh produce in Israel is mind-boggling!)

Anyway, Helene was standing towards the back of this very crowded bus, when suddenly someone tapped her on the shoulder. Years of life in Brooklyn, made Helene jump with fright.

When she heard the words, "*Geveret*, here," she turned around, and was surprised to see an older woman shoving 100 shekels into her hand.

Not knowing what the woman wanted, Helene turned back around and kept looking straight ahead.

Again the woman tapped Helene on the shoulder, and again she said, "*Geveret*, here. Take this." But this time the woman added, "A *kartisiya* [bus ticket]."

Still not quite understanding why a stranger would be handing her 100 shekels, Helene just stood there, staring, until a man reached across her and took the money from the woman.

As he passed the money on to the man in front of him, who passed it on to the child in front of him, who passed it on and on and on until the money reached the bus driver, Helene grasped what was happening — someone from the back of the crowded bus was sending money forward to buy a new bus ticket, which was good for twenty rides.

When the new bus ticket came back to Helene from the driver to the woman to the man to the man to the woman to the child to the man to the man, Helene knew what to do.

Smiling, Helene turned and passed it on, with the 62 shekels change.

And, to this day, though it happens often on the bus, Helene still hasn't forgotten her initial amazement that in Israel, people pass money back and forth through crowds of "strangers," without doubting for a moment that they will get back the correct change — with their bus tickets.

Leah

I have a friend; let's call her Leah. You probably have a few friends like her, too. She's the friend who is, well, regular. A regular, nice, kind, good, intelligent, average kind of person.

If you asked her, she would be the first to say that she isn't the one that everyone always flocks to for advice or for ideas on how to make things bigger or better or stronger. She wouldn't start a drop-in center for troubled youth, or a soup kitchen for the hungry. In fact, Leah isn't really what you think of when you imagine a "*tzadekes*" kind of person, if you know what I mean, though of course she does do *mitzvos* like all the rest of us.

Leah is just a nice, kind, good, intelligent, average kind of person.

But she did pick up and make *aliya* with her husband and three children, now grown and out of the house, a while ago, which wasn't so easy....

Leah and her family came from Brooklyn, New York, about seven years ago. And that is really when this story I want to tell started to unfold.

In America, Leah and her husband, like most Jewish families, had a periodic guest now and then who slept over. But, though she also did have guests sometimes for Shabbos and Holiday meals, they were usually friends who walked over for one meal from somewhere in the neighborhood.

However, then Leah and her family came to live in Israel, which is where Leah the Average started turning into Leah the Unbelievable, Leah the Magnificent, Leah the... well, the Unreal.

Because people from America who knew Leah started sending their children to her for a week or two when the kids were visiting in Israel. And Leah smiled, shrugged, and made them feel welcome in her three-room Jerusalem apartment.

And then the one-year girls' seminaries in Jerusalem started calling Leah every week to ask if she could "take" two or three girls from America or England "for this Shabbos" or *Chag*.

And "take," as Leah immediately learned, means complete meals and sleeping accommodations, and fresh sheets and cleaning up, and smiles, and noise and lots of activity.

But how can you say *no* when someone needs a place to eat and sleep, my friend Leah says.

So, Leah began having even more company. And more company and more company and even more company.

Because whenever the one-year-in-Israel seminaries called her, she invariably said *yes*. Thus, it didn't take the one-year-in-Israel seminaries too long to add her name to their permanent list of English-speaking host families. (Since seminaries want to show the girls who don't live here yet what a Shabbos is like in an Israeli family, they try to place their students with English-speaking families.)

And, in addition, the people who had known Leah in America kept sending their children to her "for a few days." And the neighbors of the people in America who had known her, and the co-workers of the friends and/or relatives of the people in America who had known her, and the people who had stayed with Chaya when they were in Israel, also sent *their* friends and/or relatives to stay with her for a few days when *they* were in Israel.

And, of course, concurrently, there were also the many Jerusalem neighbors and friends of Leah who lived nearby who suddenly needed extra sleeping space for a child's *aufruf* or a *sheva brachos*, as well as the neighbors who had simply overbooked their own Shabbos guests, etc., etc.

And so what has happened to my regular, ordinary, "just average" friend Leah?

Well, last week, by "accident," I got a peep into her "normal," everyday life.

She was having two one-year-in-Israel seminary students sleeping over for Shabbos, and another three one-year-in-Israel seminary girls coming for Shabbos lunch and *shalosh seudos* [the third meal], one friend of her daughter Rivky coming to sleep over and eat two meals, and one friend of her son Avi coming for the Friday evening *seuda*.

However, what made me write this article about my "just average, nothing special" friend Leah, is that she just happened to mention to me, by a slip of the tongue, that she also has for Shabbos, staying with her for over three weeks already, the daughter of a friend who used to live near her in the States.

This daughter of a friend has already been living in Leah's apartment for *more* than three weeks. She eats all of her meals with Leah's family. Leah changes her bed linen every other week, washes, dries, and folds this girl's laundry, takes the girl's telephone messages, and, are you ready for this one? Because the girl is looking for a job, she makes all of her phone calls, including long distance ones, from my friend Leah's phone, though she has never even thought of offering to pay Leah for any of them (let alone for the food she's been eating).

When I mentioned to my friend Leah that I think that she is a pretty phenomenal person, and that I know that I would certainly never be able to put up with all of the extra work and the lack of privacy and everything — especially when I didn't even know the girl — Leah, my "just regular" Leah, answered me: "Well, this girl *is* starting to be a little much. Yesterday, when I returned from work and saw her dirty dishes just sitting in the sink, I told her, 'I won't be insulted if you wash your own dishes!' I think she got the point, because she actually washed out her coffee cup and cereal bowl this morning. And she *is* looking for a job and an apartment...."

But my friend Leah still does the food shopping for her family and for all of the guests each week, and the food preparation and the cooking and the cleaning and the straightening up, and the washing and drying and laundry-folding, and all of the preparing, and, and, and... with a smile.

And that is my just average, "nothing-really-special" friend Leah.

Living in Israel. And being a "regular" Jew. While rising to greatness.

No wonder HaShem loves the People of Israel so much.

P.S. Now, when I hear the expression "being full of *mitzvos* like a pomegranate," I think of my friend Leah.

Even If You Get It Wrong

This is a story about life in Israel that even I did not believe! In fact, not only did I go over the facts two times with my daughter, whose friend had told her the story, but I even rechecked each fact twice with her friend, the protagonist, Ronit G.

Interestingly, neither my daughter nor Ronit seemed half as amazed as I was by what had happened. I guess living your whole life here in Israel does that to you....

Ronit G. is a very intelligent and capable young lady. But, being raised in Israel, I guess she was never exposed to that famous dictum that I, who was born in the

U.S., was: never, *but never,* send cash through the mail. Only send checks, and even they must be wrapped up in a piece of note-paper so that no one looking at the envelope could possibly know that there is money inside.

Well, as I mentioned, Ronit had obviously never had this Law of Life drummed into her. Because one *motzaei Shabbos* she borrowed some money from a friend and then, the next day, she returned it via the Israeli mail service, in cash, in an envelope.

The trouble was, that Ronit had not gotten her friend's address right on the front of the envelope, a fact of which Ronit was, unhappily, unaware.

However, the plot thickens, because, unbeknownst to Ronit, she had gotten something else wrong, as well. She had also written her own return address incorrectly on the envelope, since it was a new addition to her life — a post office box number.

Though Ronit had written her new post office box number correctly, she had, unwittingly, neglected to include the name of the city in which her new post office box resided.

A few weeks passed, and then, one day, Ronit got a telephone call from a woman working for the Israel Post Office.

"Are you Ronit G.?" the Israel Post Office employee asked.

When Ronit confirmed that she was, the woman announced, "We worked hard trying to find you!"

It seems that the mailman who was delivering Ronit's letter realized, while delivering the mail, that the name on the letter wasn't the correct name for the address that was written on the envelope. And it seems that he also noticed that there was cash inside the envelope.

So, not being sure that the current occupants knew to whom this letter was addressed, he returned the letter to the post office, to be returned to the sender.

However, a worker at the post office realized that there was also a mistake in the return address.

So, what did this regular Israeli postal clerk do? She started calling the post offices in each city in Israel, checking if they had a Ronit G. registered with the same post office box number that was listed in the return address on the envelope!

After many inquiries, this post office clerk finally found the correct town, and thus got Ronit's address from the post office box registration files.

However, since there was cash in that mis-addressed envelope, the post office clerk wanted to be sure.

So she looked up the phone number of the G. household in the city in which the post office box was located. And she called the phone number that was listed.

But now the problem was that the phone at Ronit's house seemed to be constantly busy during the postal clerk's working hours.

However, with persistence, the post office clerk finally got through.

Yes, the cleaning lady who came in once a week told her, this was the G. household. But Ronit lived in an apartment with some friends in another town, and the cleaning lady didn't know the address or the phone number.

So the cleaning lady gave the Israel Post Office employee the phone number of Ronit's mother, who was at work.

Reaching Ronit's mother at work, the postal clerk then got Ronit's phone number at her apartment.

And so Ronit was called by the post office worker, who was "just checking" that this was the same Ronit G. who had sent some cash through the mail.

And, since Ronit was the same person, the post office clerk got Ronit's correct current address, and then sent her back the money.

Life in Israel. Never a dull moment.

Radio Announcements

We had a huge snowfall here in Jerusalem last year.

Being Israel, by "a huge snowfall" I mean about five or six centimeters, maybe seven (around three inches) — but that is probably pushing it, and only in a snowdrift.

But, Israel being Israel, everything is special, and everything is different, here.

Which means, for starters, that of course all the areas of the country that were "hit" by the snowstorm were closed down. No traffic, no stores open, no schools open, no work for adults, no going anywhere. Just happy shouting children who romped and played in the snowdrifts all day long.

Many of the religious adults trapped at home spent at least part of the day listening to the *frum* radio stations. (Israel has several *frum* radio stations. What makes a radio station *"frum"*? First of all, any music that is played on it is, of course, only *frum* music. And *shiurim* from a variety of marvelous Rabbonim are broadcast much of the day. *Chessed* projects are periodically "advertised" for free, so that listeners can call in and offer to help. And, if any listener wants to donate some money, furniture, or other items for the needy bride or poor family being "advertised," the radio announcer, who is always male, will announce the donation on the radio.)

Towards late afternoon, when cold, dripping children were returning home from snowman-making and snowball fighting, my married daughter called to tell me what was being broadcast on all of the *frum* radio stations.

Somehow all of the *frum* radio stations

seemed to realize that, snowstorm or no snowstorm, many people already had weddings planned for that evening, which had been organized and paid for months earlier. Wedding halls, flowers, food, etc. — including excited brides and grooms, standing in happy anticipation in wedding halls waiting for guests to arrive.

But who would go out on an evening like this? And who could even *get* out with virtually no taxi-cabs or buses running?

So, what did the announcers on these *frum* radio stations do?

Starting in the late afternoon, they began announcing the time and place of all the weddings that they knew or were told about.

And they urged all young people to brave the cold and the snow and the fact that there was virtually no public transportation, and to attend these weddings. Even though they didn't know the *chassan* or the *kalla*. Or anyone in the families.

Because on a night like this, who would

go out to attend a wedding?

And can you imagine how the families would feel at an empty wedding hall with all those pre-paid, beautifully set, empty tables, and no guests?

And so the radio stations announced the time and place of wedding after wedding after wedding, and asked young people to please brave the cold and the snow and go to a wedding of people whom they didn't know.

Because it is a *mitzva* to make a bride and a groom happy on their wedding day.

Yes, many people went to weddings that night. Not just to one wedding, but to two or three or even more.

When my son-in-law returned from the wedding he had attended, he said that he had never been at a wedding that was so stuffed with people. It seems that many, many people had heard the radio announcements, and had acted on them.

What a wonderful People! And what a wonderful Land!